PEARLS
OF
WISDOM

VANESSA RODRIGO JAKUBOWSKI

Copyright © 2022 **VANESSA RODRIGO JAKUBOWSKI**

All rights reserved. This publication, or any part thereof, may not be reproduced in any form, or by any means, including electronic, photographic, or mechanical, or by any sound recording system, or by any device for storage and retrieval of information, without the written permission of the copyright owner.

Introduction

Daily Laws of Happiness

Making the most of your life is not usual - it is unusual. Most people stop learning as soon as they leave school and land their first job. However, a standard education will get you standard results - and who wants that?! Be the unusual person who keeps up the learning curve and makes the most of their life. Become a student of good ideas wherever they can be found. Every new idea you find helps refine your philosophy of life.

I have written this book to share my pearls of wisdom I have picked up along my journey, so that you can keep up the learning curve.

This book is a coffee table book - a book of daily wisdom that you can pick up to learn something new that will add value to your life.

Enjoy!

DAILY LESSONS

1.

You Are What You Eat.

All that we are is cells. Our entire body is made up of cells. And what makes up these cells is largely what we consume - food, drinks, and anything else.

When you are young, you depend on what your parents feed you. Hopefully, you have health-conscious and sensible parents who are sure to feed you a balanced diet rich in all the macronutrients, vitamins, and minerals that will help you grow healthy and strong. At a certain point, you can start to choose what you eat. Maybe you will rebel against your parents and try junk foods, sweets, alcohol, and drugs. That is your prerogative as a human being that is making their way through life and learning on the journey. Just pay attention to how things make you feel. As you get older, you may become more sensitive to things and start to gravitate toward what makes you feel better.

For example, if drinking alcohol makes you feel bad,

maybe you will do it rarely or never. If eating too much red meat or too much sugar or unrefined carbs makes you feel bloated, tired, or lacking energy, then you will naturally veer away from this.

The problem can be when people are insensitive to how things make them feel and continue with harmful or unhealthy habits to their detriment in the long run.

Just pay close attention to how the foods and drinks you consume make you feel as you move through your day, and choose accordingly.

2.

Be True to Yourself.

When things 'feel right,' and when things 'feel wrong,' they feel that way for a reason. You may have a thousand reasons to do something or not do something, but you should not go through with it if it doesn't feel right. There are a million paths you can take in life, and your instinct, or sixth sense, is your main guide in helping you to take the right ones.

When you are on a path, and it is not fulfilling anymore, have the courage to be honest and change your path. Others may not understand and may not agree, and that's OK. Live a life so courageous that you do it anyway, and live to learn the lessons and tell the tale.

3.

The First Thing To Do In The Morning ...

Is drink a big glass of water.

Water makes up 90% of our cells, and overnight we don't drink anything for around 8 hours, so we get very dehydrated. Most heart attacks happen first thing in the morning for this reason (amongst others, to do with hormones and circadian rhythms.)

Throughout the day, it is important to drink at least 7 more glasses of water. Without water, you will lack energy, lack focus, develop more issues with your skin and feel hungrier than you actually are. Many times, thirst is confused with hunger. Drink your water!

4.

The Second Thing To Do In The Morning …

Is take a walk outside.

For the first 45 minutes of the day, we are naturally primed to exert energy to burn fat. Walking is the best way to do this. Our body has a burst of natural glycogen (carbohydrates/sugar) to get the day started. After 45 minutes, it is best to eat a large, healthy, protein -packed breakfast; nevertheless, avoid refined carbohydrates such as cereal, as the body is more sensitive to refined carbs at this time.

5.

Use The Internet Responsibly.

The internet provides an entire world of information, communication, and also exposure at our fingertips. We can use this sensibly to help us with things, but we can also abuse it and end up wasting too much time, energy, and focus on stupid things. Social media (Facebook, Instagram, Twitter, TikTok, Snapchat, LinkedIn, etc.) is a great tool and can be fun and entertaining; however, you must be cautious about your use and exposure, as well as who you connect with through these channels.

Internet grooming, bullying, and scams are unfortunately all too prevalent, and although we need mobile phones and apps for everything nowadays, same way as we are cautious about what we eat and drink we need to be cautious about the internet we are consuming.

6.

Growing pains.

There will be many times in your life, especially growing up, when you feel confused, sad, frustrated, and lost. Just understand this is a normal part of growth, and always feel free to talk to your friends and family and ask for help. You should not go through things alone - your family is there to support and guide you. They've been there, done that, and got the t-shirt themselves, remember!!

7.

Confidence.

Confidence is key. Confidence that you are healthy, happy, successful, and going to achieve what you want in life. Focus on overall confidence rather than confidence in specific things. When you are generally confident versus when you are confident in one area, such as a specific sport, job, or relationship, confidence can become 'overconfidence,' which can lead to disappointment if that particular thing doesn't work out as planned. It's like a balloon that can become over-inflated and burst. When you start to feel overconfident in a specific area, rather than generally, remind yourself of the balloon analogy and soften your focus into more general confidence again.

8.

The 'reset' button.

It is common for people to abuse things in order to gain control at times when they feel negative emotions. Sometimes, people abuse food - they overeat or eat 'comfort food' during times of stress, boredom, frustration, unhappiness, etc. People also abuse alcohol, drugs, sex, pornography, exercise, fall into a spending spree, and use social media / TV and other distractions. Whilst everything can be enjoyed in moderation, you know when you are abusing something as it begins to have a negative impact on your life.

The only way I have found to avoid these things is to be disciplined and practice gratitude. Gratitude is like the 'reset 'button, which brings your emotions from negative back to positive on the scale. It will make you feel better, which will help you avoid temptations. Then discipline helps you to stay on track with every area and avoid abuse of one.

9.

Gratitude.

Gratitude is the greatest mindset trick for creating a better life immediately. Just 17 seconds of pure positive thought (such as listing what is good about your life) is the equivalent of 2000 positive action hours. More positive thoughts join the first 17 seconds, and your life is catapulted forwards positively in ways you cannot imagine.

For example, if things seem to be really terrible and everything is going wrong, you can generally start by being grateful that you woke up in the morning because, unfortunately, many people do not. You can choose to be grateful for your senses - the fact that you can see the beauty of the world, nature, the animals, and you can smell the coffee. You have family that loves you, or friends that look out for you, or your health. Even if some part of your health seems to be failing you, you can focus on the parts that are working. If your right knee is painful, focus on the left that isn't! There are always things to be grateful for. If you really make an effort to concentrate and start thinking more positive thoughts, your entire mood and attitude will shift, and so will the world around you.

10.

Relationships.

Pull back when you realise people are manipulating you for their own gain.

You will realise as you go through your life that some people seem like they have your best interests at heart, but really, what they are directing you to do benefits them as well, if not more, than you. I usually figure this out when my intuition tells me something isn't right. If you begin feeling uncomfortable around certain people, trying to avoid them or their calls, or disagreeing with what they have said, it is your internal subconscious indication that something is not right with how they are treating you. We call these people 'wolves in sheep's clothing '- meaning they appear innocent but, in reality, can be harmful.

Sometimes, close relationships with a girlfriend or a boyfriend end up like this. You will know when things just 'don't feel right' and they probably won't change or improve. Rather than waste more time and energy it's best to extricate yourself as soon as possible.

11.

Perception.

Something I learnt very early on, which has always stuck with me, is that 'people have their own map of the world.' This means that everyone has their own perspective on life. 2 people will see the same situation very differently - through their own frame of reference, through their own 'glasses.' There is not only one objective way to see things., there is not one 'truth.' A frame of reference means that people are influenced and coloured by their life experiences - what they learn, how they are raised, what media they consume, and who they are surrounded by. These influences will show up in how they are and how they see things, and what they say and do.

For example, one very simple way to spot this is work ethic. People who grow up with hard-working parents who emphasise the importance of productivity and work, as well as avoiding laziness, will usually do the same - have a good work ethic and work hard. Whereas people who have grown up around people who do not work or who do not want to work, for whatever reason, will probably avoid work.

You can see it in how people treat others who are different from them. Racism usually stems from upbringings and family and friends who are intolerant - babies are not born racist. Upbringing affects every aspect of one's life.

So if you disagree with people on things, it is not uncommon; it is common. Don't take people's opinions personally - everyone just simply has their own map of the world.

12.

Embracing failure.

'I have not failed. I have just found 10,000 ways that won't work'.

Thomas Edison

Failure doesn't feel good. You have confidence in something, and it doesn't work. Maybe people are counting on you, and you let them down. Maybe you are counting on yourself, and you feel like giving up; however, try to remember - when you fail or lose, it is only because there is something better available. There is a better way, a better relationship, a better job, a better way to do it. The failure is telling you there is an opportunity for expansion and growth. Accept it.

13.

Procrastination.

Don't make the mistake of leaving all the things you want to do until tomorrow. Any changes you want to make, you need to put them into action today. Even if it is the smallest step, even if it is just making the decision to make the change, do it today if you are called towards it.

14.

Motion = Emotion.

Make sure that exercise in some form is part of your daily routine. Not only does exercise have many health benefits, but motion also creates emotion. When you get moving, you can guarantee that when you get back home, you will feel better.

15.

Wash away stress.

If you feel stressed, take a shower and wash your hair, or even better, go for a swim in a pool or sea and get your head submerged. Water running over your head is one of the most energetically cleansing things you can do and will help you feel less stressed.

16.

Self mastery.

Master yourself before you look for a relationship to complete you.

17.

Spending money.

Choose to view spending money as circulating currency. That way, more is likely to come to you! If you begrudge spending a penny, money will be hard to come by.

18.

Bright ideas.

Write down all of your good ideas, thoughts, and inspirations in a daily journal or notepad. You never know if these ideas will turn into a product that improves humanity, a best-seller that makes you a lot of money or a book that makes you famous!

19.

Learning.

Learn something new every day - grow the brain, expand the mind, and stay curious and interested. There is always more to learn, and the funny thing is, the more we learn the more we realise we don't know!

When we learn, important changes happen in the brain, including the creation of new connections between your neuron's. This is called neuroplasticity. The more you practice, the stronger these connections become, and the more able you are to learn new things!

20.

Sleep.

Get a good night's sleep - sleep is very, very important to repair, rest and grow.

There are many negative effects of poor sleep, including effects on your digestive systems, immune system, cardiovascular system, endocrine system, respiratory system and central nervous system.

If you are suffering, talk to you doctor as you may have a sleep disorder that you can get help with.

21.

Marriage.

You don't have to marry your childhood sweetheart!

As much as you may have a first love, and definitely feel like you love them and you will be with them forever, people change a lot in their 20s. Some change together, and some change apart. Be careful not to rush into your first marriage or it may not be your last!

22.

Reality.

Remember - you don't FACE reality; you create reality.

Life may seem like it is happening to you, and you have very little control, but in fact the opposite is true. Every belief you hold in the 30 trillion cells in your body (that's a recent scientist estimate) will show itself play out to you, in your reality, sooner or later.

Choose your beliefs carefully!

23.

Attention.

Be aware of where you focus your conscious attention stream - for example, the news. Negative news influences negative streams of thought. Disqualify those streams by focusing on the positive and wanting more positive than negative outcomes.

24.

Narcissism.

Identify and dismiss narcissistic people in your life before they do too much damage. These people will masquerade as having your best intentions in mind but actually manipulate you to ensure you are under their control and they get what they want. You can never beat a narcissist.

25.

Purpose driven living.

We must figure out what our purpose is in life. Just doing things for money will likely lead you to unhappiness. Money will likely be the indirect outcome of working for a higher purpose, such as helping others or changing lives. Same as companies have a guiding philosophy that fuels their everyday actions, you must have your guiding philosophy. We all have a purpose for being here, and if we pay attention long enough we can work it out.

26.

Thinking .v. doing.

Remember to give yourself time to think (don't stay too busy) every day - but not too much time! Be productive as well - the devil creates work for idle hands and idle minds!

27.

Stories.

The stories you tell are the communities you build. How you speak and what you speak about will influence who wants to be around you. Negative stories will bring negative people, and vice versa.

28.

The benefit of hindsight.

Life only makes sense in hindsight - when looking back. So as long as you have faith and know in which direction you are headed - and enter your destination like you would on satellite navigation system - although you may have right and left turns and twists and turns on the way, you can trust you will reach the destination.

29.

Remembrance.

When you reach your destination, remember the days you wished for what you now have, and remember to be grateful for how far you have come and how much you have achieved. There will always be contrast and more to chase, but remember gratitude before greed.

30.

Focus on the positives.

We always want to focus on what is going right rather than what is going wrong. If you have 5 areas of life you focus on daily - money, career, family, health & relationship, for example, and one of those areas has taken a turn for the worst, rather than worrying incessantly about that area, try to focus on the other areas that are going right. This will provide you with some light relief and time to figure out how to improve the area that is going wrong.

31.

Posture.

Posture is incredibly important, especially if you are sitting at a desk all day. Remember daily to focus on it and use a light resistance band to open up your shoulders. In the gym, make sure to utilise the 'face pull' exercise and do a pull-focused session a minimum of twice a week to strengthen the back and keep your shoulders sitting on top of your shoulder blades in the right position. Otherwise, you can be at risk of hyper-kyphosis (hump back.)

32.

Stand tall.

Standing tall and straight is very important to send out signals of confidence and avoid sending out victim signals.

33.

Breathe.

Breathing correctly, through your nose, is very important. Mouth breathing is incorrect and is responsible for a lot of respiratory and cranio-facial development issues. Sleep issues such as sleep apnea, insomnia, anxiety, stress and panic attacks will be improvedby learning to breathe effectively through your nose. Your nose is for breathing, the mouth is for eating and speaking!

34.

Hurt people.

As you move through life, remember that hurt people, hurt people. There will be times when other people do and say very nasty, cutting things. Don't take it personally. Don't let it knock your confidence. People who are happy in themselves are not trying to hurt other people. People who are hurt or suffering insecurity are likely to do that to try and help themselves feel better.

35.

Life philosophy.

You cannot hear the fundamentals of life philosophy too often. They are the greatest form of nutrition - the building blocks for a well-developed mind. You won't learn them in school, so you have to make sure you learn them through books by well-known philosophers.

36.

Look for love.

Look for something you love! Every time you look in the mirror, out of the window, or at other people. Look through rose-tinted glasses; it will only help you feel better.

37.

Growth.

There is always room to grow. There is always more knowledge to gain and more skills to perfect. We are never finished with the education process because education is part of the path to wealth and the path to health. Continued education can turn you around if you are headed in the wrong direction. We must never stop growing and expanding.

38.

The Comfort Zone.

Living in your comfort zone can lead to feelings of boredom and frustration, which are a certain kind of stress, due to not feeling challenged regularly. Living outside of your comfort zone leads to all kinds of stress that comes from being challenged by new things you haven't experienced before. Everyone will have their own preference, but my worst fear is the comfort zone, because I know I will not grow and develop as a person if I am living in my comfort zone.

39.

Children.

Focus on the needs of children rather than the behaviour of children. This can help adults and caregivers assist the child in the correct way rather than punishing them for expressing their needs.

40.

The truth.

Remember that the truth will only present itself under compassionate enquiry - only when compassion is present do people feel comfortable to reveal themselves and the truth.

41.

Physical connection.

Increase physical connections. In this day and age with the rise of technology and social media, it it easy to go days without seeing another human being. However, social interactions are vital in order to stave off loneliness and physical diseases that come from too much time alone with screens.

42.

Happiness.

Real happiness doesn't come from external material items like cars or watches. Real happiness comes from spending your time doing productive things that interest you, motivate you and allow you to earn a living. Having time freedom and financial freedom to the extent that you can pay for your life without having to spend every day miserable at your work.

43.

You are valuable.

Remember that you are valuable and what you have to say is valuable.

44.

Rest.

Don't beat yourself up for taking a break and taking some rest. All themotivational 'gurus 'preach that you are not doing enough unless you wake up at 4am in the morning and get in a workout, read, write, plan your day, go through your goals and meditate before you go to work. In reality, we only have a set amount of motivation& energy every day, so when your focus runs out, don't beat yourself up for having to rest!

45.

Your dreams.

Dream big!! Your dreams should make people feel uncomfortable because they expand energy and consciousness. Be a creator and visionary!

46.

Feeling uncomfortable.

If something makes you feel uncomfortable, it is because it makes you behave against your soul and true source. You don't have to do it!

47.

What others think.

Don't work against yourself by worrying about what people think of you. Be kind to yourself. We cannot control what other people think, regardless of how hard we try to be a 'nice person 'or agree with others, or 'play nicely 'with others.

48.

Emotional balance.

Keep your emotional balance by judging people by their actions and not taking them personally. You have to be able to look at life like moves on a chessboard. If someone does something 'nasty' to you, don't get upset - stay neutral and imagine it's like being punched in the boxing ring - it is part of the game!

49.

Stay Disciplined.

True happiness comes from knowing what you want to achieve and doing what is necessary to get there. If you want to improve your health, for example, there are clear ways to do this and only by staying disciplined and following these methods will you achieve the better health you desire. There is no such thing as cheating - you will either stay disciplined and achieve your goals or not.

50.

The rule of 5.

Don't sweat the small stuff - if it won't matter in 5 years, don't spend more than 5 minutes stressing about it.

51.

Hold space.

Hold space for yourself. Don't feel intimidated or shy by people who hold more space for themselves. Stand tall and match it.

52.

Discipline.

The things that are the easiest to do and also the easiest things not to do. Doing something everyday and not doing something everyday will both add up and compound over time - the things you do do, can lead to a successful life. The things you fail to do can also lead to an unsuccessful life.

53.

Food cravings.

One of the easiest ways to stay healthy and keep your food cravings under control is to simply not keep foods that you don't want to eat in your house. No matter how disciplined you are, if you have food in your kitchen, you are way more inclined to eat it! Make life easier for yourself by only having food that you want to eat accessible!

54.

Head or heart?

In all battles between your heart and your head, choose your heart. The head will catch up!

55.

Making comparisons.

Health is particularly corroded by looking at things you do not have, which you wish to have. Therefore be careful with the social media you pay attention to, as looking at highly curated and edited lifestyles can cause negative feelings of comparison!

56.

Family practice.

Create a family gratitude journal and open conversations about what you are grateful for in each other.

57.

Celebrate yourself.

Choose to celebrate yourself rather than beat yourself up! There are enough other people who will do that for you!

58.

Consumption.

Remember that 'consumption' is not just food. It is food, drinks, alcohol, drugs, the kind of information you listen to and also read. What you consume is who you are. Be a careful consumer!

59.

Life is an adventure.

Every day, you have the chance to write another page of your adventure book. Life doesn't have to be a simple rat race of education, work, paying bills and retiring. You have the power to choose your life adventure. Don't believe in limits!

60.

Self interest.

When dealing with others at school or work, remember that people operate from self-interest. Whenever delivering anything, always ask yourself, 'what is in it for them? '

61.

Learn another language.

Becoming proficient in a second language really keeps the brain active and flexible to take more information. Language is the key to so many opportunities.

62.

Smile.

'If you have good thoughts, they will shine out of your face like sunbeams, and you will always look lovely. '

Roald Dahl

63.

Meditate.

Rather than waking up with an alarm and rushing around first thing, taking time to meditate for just 5 minutes each morning helps to quiet the mind and connect with the body, ready for a positive and successful day ahead. You can find many free guided meditations online.

64.

Beliefs.

The world we believe in becomes the world we live in. If you see something you don't like, choose to look away and think less about it rather than focus in on it. This way it won't expand in your world.

65.

Courage.

Just getting through the day - let alone reaching for the stars - requires courage. True courage is a priceless commodity. Many people are afraid of what might happen to them financially, or to their health, or to their family. The truth is, great changes are continuously happening in the economy that has a direct impact on millions of lives. We have chemicals in our food, and the price of healthy staples like chicken and fruit is increasing, and if you are in a country like America, the cost of getting sick and not having insurance is unfathomable. What we need to do is accept responsibility for our circumstances and our future and realise we cannot rely on anybody to look out for us.

66.

Envy.

Make envy a spur to achievement - instead of wanting to hurt or steal from the person you are envious of, we should desire to raise ourselves to his or her level. We cannot stop the comparing mechanism in our brains, so it is best to redirect it into something productive and creative.

67.

Your experience shapes you.

Be sure to be grateful to have experienced a journey like yours. Always remember the process will become your story. The story that is capable of bringing out the best in others! You cannot create the experience - you must go through it!

68.

Being strong.

A strong body = a strong mind, and vice versa! Treating your body and your mind with respect should be a priority to feel your best in every way, every day.

69.

Humans are remarkable.

'Humans can turn nothing into something, pennies into fortune, disaster into success. The reason we can do such remarkable things is because we are remarkable.'

(*Leading an inspired life*, Jim Rohn)

70.

Work.

Most traditional working environments are very unnatural (offices with harsh lighting, lack of proper ventilation, surrounded all day, every day by hostile and competitive people and staring at a screen, or 2) which can cause a lot of stress. Some people can navigate these waters better than others and so will be able to 'climb the career ladder.' Others, however, will not and will find another way to survive. You will find out for yourself as you experience these things what is true for you.

71.

Less is more.

The more you have, the more you have to lose. Sometimes maintaining things are more difficult than acquiring in the first place! The best way is to keep life light and moderate. Less baggage means less stress.

72.

The Universe.

Every morning, when you leave the house, look up to the sky and say, 'dear universe, show me how good it gets today.'

73.

Challenges.

View every challenge is an opportunity to get better.

74.

Happiness over unhappiness.

Remember that we cannot be happy and unhappy at the same time. One will take precedence over the other. So pick one for any reason. You can pick happiness and pick one reason to be happy, focus on that, and unhappiness gets locked out.

75.

Don't bite the hand that feeds you.

This may seem obvious, but it is remarkably easy to get comfortable in a situation and stop appreciating where your blessings are coming from. For example, we are so grateful to have a well paying job, but before long we start complaining about our colleagues, our boss or the working conditions. Or we are excited to build a new business and we are grateful every time we land a new client, but before long we are complaining that we are too busy, the hours are too long and we stop appreciating our clients. This is the fastest way to losing what you were once grateful for. Remember, as quickly as it came it can disappear.

76.

Invest wisely.

Don't only work for money - make your money work for you. There are a multiple of ways you can cleverly invest your money. However, be careful as there are thousands of ruthless scammers who will strip you of your last penny and not look back!

77.

Solving problems.

Remember, when facing a problem or challenge - the bigger and worse the problem, the more delicious it is when you align yourself with the answer!

78.

Prioritise health.

For a balanced and healthy approach to life, and to feel as good as possible, we need to prioritise eating sufficient protein (the building blocks of muscles, bones, organs, skin, and nails), carbohydrates (provide the body with glucose, which is converted to energy used to support bodily functions and physical activity), and healthy fats (support cell function, protect organs, keep your body warm, help your body absorb nutrients and produce important hormones)

79.

Laugh & cry.

There is a time to laugh and a time to cry. While laughter may be more desirable, it's important to learn to cry well, too.

80.

Comparison.

If you are going to compare yourself to anyone, compare yourself to those who have less, not more, than you have and consider how lucky you are.

81.

Learn which colours suit your skin tone.

Wearing the right and wrong colours can massively impact how you look and how you come across to others. There is an abundance of information about which colours suit which hair and skin tones best, but also just looking at pictures of yourself wearing different colours will prove to you which really flatter you and which dull you down.

82.

Failure.

'There's no failure in pouring your heart and soul and energy into something that doesn't work. Rather, failure is not trying at all.'

(*Leading an inspired life*, Jim Rohn)

83.

Taking advice.

People may be looking out for your best intentions, however we all have our own journey and path we need to follow in life. You can ask for and listen to advice but if you disagree with it you don't have to follow it.

84.

'You need to do more than just eat nourish food, exercise and rest to feel your best. You also need to be around good people, spend time healing your emotional history, live in alignment with your values, say no to people pleasing, stay open to growth and deeply embrace change.'

~ Yung Pueblo

85.

Physicality.

We need to combine both weight training and aerobic (cardiovascular) exercise each week to be as fit, healthy and strong as possible.

Weight training is crucial to build muscle, which protects our joints and helps us feel stronger, improves bone health, increases our energy levels, improves mood, elevates our body image, enhances our brain health and gives us better flexibility and mobility.

Aerobic (cardiovascular exercise) is key for a strong and healthy heart, fat burn, improving stamina, keeping your arteries clear, boosting your mood and keeping excess weight off.

86.

Control your emotions.

In terms of your emotions, you have to see yourself as the rider and your emotions as the horse. You can't let your emotions ride you!

87.

The Greatest Teacher.

Life is the greatest teacher. You don't have to listen, but if you don't, the same lesson will come around many times in many forms. If things aren't going your way, you have to sit down and analyse where your actions and behaviours are making things go wrong. There is no blame outside of yourself. Try to learn quickly!

88.

Gut instincts.

Trust your gut instinct about people. They never lie. They are your subconscious protection mechanism.

89.

Always ask for what you want.

If you do not ask, the answer will always be no.

90.

Push yourself forward.

Do not be shy; push yourself forwards.

91.

Networking.

Most business happens outside of the office. If you are in a job where business connections are important, to view your time in the office / at work as the only time to increase connections and / or improve the strength of relationships is wrong.

92.

You are special.

Never fail to have confidence in your talents - the special and unique strengths you bring to the world. You may not be able to see them yourself, but others will definitely be able to tell you where your power lies. Be cool, be confident in what you bring to the table. We are all created unique - let the world see you stand tall in who you are because we are all special!

93.

Be Strategic.

In life you will come up against opponents who may be stronger, faster or more intelligent than you. Like in a football game, not every team has an even chance of winning. Some teams are obviously better players than their opponents. However, that doesn't mean they will always win. If the weaker team have a stronger strategy in place, they have more chance of winning. If you study your opposition and have a better strategy in place, it is likely to pay off.

94.

Explore.

How to view the world - see yourself as an explorer. You explore all forms of knowledge from all cultures and time periods. You want to be challenged.

95.

Consistency.

You have to be disciplined in creating consistent positive habits. Daily tasks like brushing your teeth are easy to be consistent with, because they have become an integral part of your daily routine for many many years. Even if you are a inconsistent person generally, you can be consistent in your positive habits, such as exercise & eating properly.

96.

Change.

Wherever you go, you take yourself with you! This means change doesn't come from moving to a different place, being in a different job or being in a different relationship. Change comes from within.

97.

Life's waves.

In life, you will have 'impulse waves 'and 'corrective waves'. Impulse waves are when things move forward quickly, things seem to be going really well, and the tide moves forward in a positive manner. Corrective waves are when life pulls you back a bit and reminds you that you are only human and to remain humble. When going through corrective wave remember it won't last forever, keep pushing forward!

98.

The laws of the universe.

If the laws of the universe are unknown to you or misunderstood, or you are not good at applying them, then you won't get good results, because words don't teach. Others who have had good results can demonstrate all day every day that they do, but as you watch from your vantage point of not knowing, you want to trust and believe - you watch others, and it teaches you that they have good success, not necessarily that you can too. But when you start focusing on the laws of the universe and develop your own patterns of applying the laws of the universe, you will notice your own vibrational point of attraction and contouring your own frequency. You begin thinking about deliberately choosing the frequency before you apply it to thought. You gain control from the early stages rather than waiting for it to occur, and you control the momentum early on.

99.

Manifestation.

There is nothing more satisfying than thinking of something you want, knowing you don't have it yet but believing it is coming in time because you know what to do between now and its manifestation in order to bring it along.

100.

Men are from Mars.

Men are very simple creatures. Women are far more complex. For women to attract men, they need to understand that men only have the ability to focus on only one thing at a time. They can only have one primary focus. So if you are attracted to a man, and his eyes are set on his primary focus, the difficulty is getting yourself as his primary focus. How you get his attention is through physicality and then building a connection through having things in common. The conversation won't go very far if you are both into completely different things. You have to have common ground. Once he becomes interested in your personality, you can begin a sexual relationship.

101.

When you can't sleep.

Sometimes I find my mind racing when the world is quiet and I am trying to fall asleep. All the worries, doubts and bad memories seem to boil up to the surface. The best way I have found to counteract these troublesome thoughts, rather than count sheep or count backwards, is just to repeat the words 'thank you' over and over in my head. It soothes the soul, and helps me fall asleep quickly!

www.ingramcontent.com/pod-product-compliance
Lightning Source LLC
Chambersburg PA
CBHW070240220526
45465CB00004B/1469